JUMP!

RABBITS AND HARES

Lynette Robbins

PowerKiDS press
New York

For Claire

Published in 2012 by The Rosen Publishing Group, Inc.
29 East 21st Street, New York, NY 10010

First Edition

Editor: Joanne Randolph
Book Design: Ashley Drago and Erica Clendening

Photo Credits: Cover, p. 8 Jorgen Larsson/Getty Images; p. 4 Design Pics/The Irish Image Collection/Valueline/Thinkstock; pp. 5, 7 (bottom), 12–13, 17 (top), 18, 20 Shutterstock.com; pp. 6, 21, 22 Hemera/Thinkstock; p. 7 (top) Tom Brakefield/Getty Images; p. 9 (top) Design Pics/David Ponton/Valueline/Thinkstock; pp. 9 (bottom), 14, 17 (bottom) iStockphoto/Thinkstock; pp. 10–11 © ARCO/Usher D/age fotostock; p. 15 (top) John & Barbara Gerlach/Getty Images; p. 15 (bottom) Jeremy Woodhouse/Getty Images; p. 16 Tom Brakefield/Stockbyte/Thinkstock; p. 19 Beverly Joubert/Getty Images.

Library of Congress Cataloging-in-Publication Data

Robbins, Lynette.
  Rabbits and hares / by Lynette Robbins. — 1st ed.
     p. cm. — (Jump!)
  Includes index.
  ISBN 978-1-4488-5018-1 (library binding) — ISBN 978-1-4488-5169-0 (pbk.) —
ISBN 978-1-4488-5170-6 (6-pack)
  1. Rabbits—Juvenile literature. 2. Hares—Juvenile literature. I. Title. II. Series.
  QL737.L32R63 2012
  599.32—dc22

2011004913

Manufactured in the United States of America

CPSIA Compliance Information: Batch #WS11PK: For Further Information contact Rosen Publishing, New York, New York at 1-800-237-9932

Contents

Hello, Hare! Greetings, Rabbit!

Have you ever seen a rabbit in the wild? Maybe it was eating some grass in your yard. Maybe you saw one while you were walking in the woods. Even if you think you saw a rabbit, it might not have been a rabbit at all! It might have been a hare. Rabbits and hares

Scientists think that one of the reasons rabbits have long ears is to help them hear predators, or animals that want to eat them.

look almost the same. They both have long ears and soft fur. Both rabbits and hares are powerful jumpers.

Rabbits and hares are part of the same **family** of animals. They are also related to pikas. Pikas are much smaller than rabbits and hares, and they do not have long ears.

Hares, such as this one, generally have longer legs than rabbits do.

Hare, There, and Everywhere

Rabbits and hares live in almost every part of the world. They can live on cold, snowy mountains or in hot, dry deserts. Both rabbits and hares can be found on grassy plains and in fields where crops grow.

Rabbits dig burrows with many dens and tunnels that connect to each other. A large group of rabbit burrows is

This rabbit makes its home in the desert. It needs to move around a lot to find enough food in this dry place.

called a **warren**. Rabbits like to dig their burrows in sandy soil where there are some trees and shrubs.

Hares do not dig burrows. They make body-shaped hollows in the grass, called **forms**. Hares live in open places such as plains, **tundras**, and deserts.

ABOVE: Snowshoe hares live in cold places. In the winter their fur turns white to help them blend in with their snowy surroundings.

LEFT: Rabbits dig burrows in the ground where they stay during the day. They come out in the evenings or at night to eat.

What's the Difference?

Do you know the difference between a rabbit and a hare? They are different in several ways. Hares are bigger than rabbits. Hares can weigh up to 15 pounds (7 kg) while the largest rabbits in the wild weigh only about 5 pounds (2 kg). Hares have longer legs and longer ears than rabbits do. Hares also have black-tipped ears.

This hare has black on the ends of its ears. This is one way to tell rabbits and hares apart.

LEFT: Cottontails are one of the best-known kinds of rabbits in the United States. They get their name from their white tails, which look like pieces of cotton.

BELOW: Jackrabbits, such as this one, are really hares. They have very long ears, long legs, and can jump away from danger quickly.

Most rabbits and hares are brown or gray. Some kinds can turn white during the winter to blend in with the snow.

There are 56 **species** of rabbits and hares. Some of these include cottontails, snowshoe hares, and jackrabbits. Even though they are called rabbits, jackrabbits are really hares!

9

Bouncing Bunnies and Hopping Hares

Rabbits and hares are known for their jumping. They have long, strong back legs. Rabbits and hares jump by bringing their back legs up beside their front legs. Then they spring up.

A rabbit or hare can jump up to 20 feet (6 m) in a single bounce. Hares are faster than rabbits. Some kinds of hares

can jump more than 40 miles per hour (64 km/h)! Rabbits are slower, so they often try to trick their **predators** rather than outrun them. Rabbits confuse their predators by changing directions with each jump.

Hares use their strong back legs to jump. They hop to get away from enemies. Males may also hop when they are trying to win over females for mating.

Rabbit and Hare Facts

4

Some kinds of rabbits and hares make a high-pitched scream when they are scared.

5

Rabbits and hares that live in cold places have shorter ears than those of rabbits and hares that live in warm places.

6

The snowshoe hare really does have snowshoes! It has mats of fur on the bottoms of its feet that allow it to walk on soft snow without sinking.

A female rabbit or hare is called a doe. A male is called a buck.

1

The antelope jackrabbit has ears that are nearly one-third the length of its body!

2

Mother rabbits hide their babies, or kittens, in secret burrows. This is because they do not want male rabbits to find the kittens. Male rabbits will kill babies that are not their own.

3

7

The smallest rabbit is the pygmy rabbit. It weighs less than 1 pound (454 g).

8

Many people keep **domestic** rabbits as pets. Some domestic rabbits have been bred to be bigger than wild rabbits. Some have also been bred to have floppy ears. Wild rabbits never have floppy ears.

9

Rabbits are not **native** to Australia and New Zealand. People brought a few rabbits to these countries. The rabbits multiplied quickly. Soon there were so many that they became pests.

It's Time to Eat!

Rabbits and hares are **herbivores.** That means they eat only plants. Rabbits and hares eat mostly grasses and clovers. They also eat other plants, such as flowers and weeds. When dining on bigger plants, they may eat just part of the plant, such as the twigs, bark, seeds, or buds. Hares get most of the water they need from the plants

When rabbits and hares first start eating, they quickly eat any plants they can find. After a while, they start eating more slowly and pick some plants over others.

14

LEFT: This black-tailed jackrabbit is standing on its back legs to eat leaves and flowers from a creosote bush. Black-tailed jackrabbits live in deserts.

BELOW: Rabbits drink from bodies of water by lapping the water with their tongues, much as dogs or cats do.

they eat. Sometimes they eat snow if they need more water in the wintertime.

Have you ever read the story about Peter Rabbit getting into Mr. McGregor's garden? Just like Peter, real rabbits and hares love vegetables! Rabbits and hares can ruin gardens or farm crops.

Plenty of Predators

Rabbits and hares have many predators. Weasels, foxes, coyotes, badgers, and bobcats eat rabbits and hares. Danger is not just on the ground, either. Birds such as owls, hawks, buzzards, crows, and ravens dive down from the sky to **prey** on rabbits and hares, too.

Hares count on their quickness to get away from predators. When a hare sees or hears a predator, it jumps

This snowshoe hare is running from a hungry mountain lion. Hares, like this one, make it possible for many larger meat eaters to live.

away fast! When a rabbit senses a predator, it thumps both its back legs on the ground to warn other rabbits nearby. When the rabbits hear the warning, they all run toward whichever burrow is the closest.

LEFT: Rabbits and hares have to be careful of pets such as dogs trying to catch them. Some people hunt rabbits using dogs, too.

BELOW: This wedge-tailed eagle has caught a rabbit. The wedge-tailed eagle is a predator of small animals in Australia.

Alone or Together

Although they are both **nocturnal**, rabbits and hares live very different lives. Hares live alone. They eat in the evening. During the day, they rest in their forms. Hares stay still in their forms so that predators will not see them. They are always ready to jump, though.

Rabbits are more likely to be seen in groups than are hares, but even hares sometimes eat in the same field as other hares.

Rabbits spend their days inside their burrows. At night, they come out to feed. Rabbits do not go far from their burrows. They use their front paws to loosen dirt to dig their burrows. Then they kick the loose dirt away with their strong back legs.

Hares in their forms count on blending in with their surroundings. They hold very still to keep from being seen by hungry animals.

Kittens and Leverets

A female rabbit gives birth in a nest that she makes in her burrow. She may have three to nine kittens at a time. The newborn kittens are very small with almost no fur. They are blind and deaf. They cannot move until they are 10 days old. After about 16 days, they are ready to leave the nest.

ABOVE AND RIGHT: Baby rabbits spend around two weeks in their nests. Many babies do not live that long, though. This is partly why mother rabbits have so many babies each year.

Female hares have up to six babies at a time. A baby hare is called a leveret. Leverets can hop around a few minutes after they are born. Each leveret makes its own form. Every day the mother hare visits each form to **nurse** the leverets.

Hare Today, Gone Tomorrow

People sometimes hunt rabbits and hares for their meat and fur or just for sport. Farmers sometimes kill them so they will not eat their crops. Pet dogs and cats also kill rabbits and hares.

Most species of rabbits and hares are not **endangered**. However, a few species are in danger of becoming **extinct**. The tiny volcano rabbit lives in the mountains in Mexico. The hispid hare lives in the foothills of the Himalayas. The riverine rabbit lives in the desert in South Africa. These species

Rabbits and hares can eat a lot of plants in one day. This is why farmers are not always happy to have them living on their farms and sharing their crops.

are endangered because people are destroying their **habitats** by chopping down the trees and grazing farm animals where these rabbits and hares like to live. Rabbits and hares are an important part of the ecosystem. Let's hope they are hopping around for a long time to come.

Glossary

domestic (duh-MES-tik) Having to do with animals made by people picking which animals to breed together.

endangered (in-DAYN-jerd) In danger of no longer existing.

extinct (ik-STINGKT) No longer existing.

family (FAM-lee) The scientific name for a large group of plants or animals that are alike in some ways.

forms (FORMZ) Hares' resting places.

habitats (HA-buh-tats) The surroundings in which animals or plants naturally live.

herbivores (ER-buh-vorz) Animals that eat only plants.

native (NAY-tiv) Born or grown in a certain place or country.

nocturnal (nok-TUR-nul) Active during the night.

nurse (NURS) When a female feeds her baby milk from her body.

predators (PREH-duh-terz) Animals that kill other animals for food.

prey (PRAY) To hunt for food.

species (SPEE-sheez) One kind of living thing. All people are one species.

tundras (TUN-druz) The frozen land of the coldest parts of the world.

warren (WAWR-en) A group of connecting underground tunnels and dens built by rabbits.

Index

C

crops, 6, 15, 22

D

danger, 16, 22

desert(s), 6–7, 22

E

ears, 5, 8, 12–13

F

form(s), 7, 18, 21

fur, 5, 12, 20, 22

G

grass(es), 4, 7, 14

L

leveret(s), 21

M

mountains, 6, 22

P

people, 13, 22

predator(s), 11, 16–18

T

tunnels, 6

Web Sites

Due to the changing nature of Internet links, PowerKids Press has developed an online list of Web sites related to the subject of this book. This site is updated regularly. Please use this link to access the list:
www.powerkidslinks.com/jump/rabbits/